T0334572

Cambridge Elements ≡

Elements in Law, Economics and Politics

Series Editor in Chief
Carmine Guerriero, *University of Bologna*

Series Co-Editors
Alessandro Riboni, *École Polytechnique*
Jillian Grennan, *Duke University, Fuqua School of Business*
Petros Sekeris, *Montpellier Business School*

DEEP IV IN LAW

Appellate Decisions and Texts Impact Sentencing in Trial Courts

Zhe Huang
Tufts University
Xinyue Zhang
OpenX
Ruofan Wang
Microsoft
Daniel L. Chen
Toulouse 1 Capitole University

CAMBRIDGE
UNIVERSITY PRESS

CAMBRIDGE
UNIVERSITY PRESS

University Printing House, Cambridge CB2 8BS, United Kingdom

One Liberty Plaza, 20th Floor, New York, NY 10006, USA

477 Williamstown Road, Port Melbourne, VIC 3207, Australia

314–321, 3rd Floor, Plot 3, Splendor Forum, Jasola District Centre,
New Delhi – 110025, India

103 Penang Road, #05–06/07, Visioncrest Commercial, Singapore 238467

Cambridge University Press is part of the University of Cambridge.

It furthers the University's mission by disseminating knowledge in the pursuit of education, learning, and research at the highest international levels of excellence.

www.cambridge.org
Information on this title: www.cambridge.org/9781009296373
DOI: 10.1017/9781009296403

© Zhe Huang, Xinyue Zhang, Ruofan Wang, and Daniel L. Chen 2022

First published 2022

A catalogue record for this publication is available from the British Library.

ISBN 978-1-009-29637-3 Paperback

ISSN 2732-4931 (online)
ISSN 2732-4923 (print)

Deep IV in Law

Appellate Decisions and Texts Impact Sentencing in Trial Courts

Elements in Law, Economics and Politics

DOI: 10.1017/9781009296403
First published online: July 2022

The co-editors in charge of this submission were Carmine Guerriero and Rosa Ferrer

Zhe Huang
Tufts University

Xinyue Zhang
OpenX

Ruofan Wang
Microsoft

Daniel L. Chen
Toulouse 1 Capitole University

Author for correspondence: Daniel L. Chen, daniel.chen@tse-fr.eu

Abstract: Do US Circuit Courts' decisions on criminal appeals influence sentence lengths imposed by US District Courts? This Element explores the use of high-dimensional instrumental variables to estimate this causal relationship. Using judge characteristics as instruments, this Element implements two-stage models on court sentencing data for the years 1991 through 2013. This Element finds that Democratic, Jewish judges tend to favor criminal defendants, while Catholic judges tend to rule against them. This Element also finds from experiments that prosecutors backlash to circuit court rulings while district court judges comply. Methodologically, this Element demonstrates the applicability of deep instrumental variables to legal data.

Keywords: legal data, causal inference, natural language processing, machine learning, Deep IV

ISBNs: 9781009296373 (PB), 9781009296403 (OC)
ISSNs: 2732-4931 (online), 2732-4923 (print)

Contents

1 Introduction

This Element develops a method for conducting automated impact analyses of court precedent and applies it to criminal sentencing. This topic has received much attention due to the massive build-up of prisons in the US criminal justice system. We apply methods from machine learning, natural language processing, and causal inference to measure the causal impact of criminal appeal decisions in circuit courts.

Legal theorists and historians have long debated the proper relationship between constitutional law and politics. While some have argued that judicial decision-making should be political (Schmitt 1969, 1985, 2005), most scholars have emphasized the importance of separation from political interests. Debates over the political role of the judiciary have intensified in recent years. This Element assesses the impacts of ideological motivations of United States US federal judges as reflected in their rulings and subsequent compliance by federal courts as evidence that this debate over judicial decision-making has consequences. We test the effects of legal precedent in criminal justice on subsequent sentencing decisions of district court judges and sentencing charges by federal prosecutors.

To conduct our analysis, we represent the text of judicial decisions as data. We then take these text features, along with metadata about the judges and case facts, to predict appeal court decisions (affirm/reverse) and district court sentencing decisions (length of sentence, in months). Using a high-dimensional instrumental variables approach, we measure the causal relations underlying these processes.

Our approach is based on Hartford and colleagues (2017). The prediction problem is divided into a two-stage model. In the first stage, we fit models that learn to predict appeal decisions of the circuit court as well as the vector representation of judge opinion text, where the instruments include characteristics of assigned judges. Intuitively, the Deep IV methods will be beneficial in predicting a high-dimensional embedding vector describing the text features of the written decision. In the second stage, we predict district court sentencing length decisions. These models use the first-stage predictions as inputs, so the resulting model parameters have a causal interpretation. We compare these Deep IV predictions to the noncausal Deep ordinary least squares (OLS) predictions and the Deep Reduced Form predictions that use only the judge characteristics as regressors. We also report feature importance and OLS coefficients. The reduced form model is used to substantiate causality and aid in interpretability.

We find that an appeal case that affirms a lower-court crime decision (i.e., a decision to be harsh) is followed by a statistically significant increase in sentencing percentile relative to sentencing guidelines in the lower courts of that circuit. However, there is a statistically insignificant effect on sentence lengths. Sentence guidelines dictating the minimum and maximum are based on a formula using the prosecutor's charge. We therefore interpret these results as being due to the interplay of prosecutors and judges, where prosecutors backlash to circuit rulings by issuing more lenient charges after a harsh ruling (or, conversely, harsh charges after a lenient ruling), yet district judges are largely obeying the circuit rulings. This is consistent with the growing attention to the large role for discretion in decision-making by prosecutors.

2 Theoretical Framework

There is an extensive research literature on the topic of judicial decision-making and sentencing. And it is clear that contextual factors related to political, judicial, and social environments affect prison sentences (Huang et al. 1996). Regional variation in sentencing has been documented in a lot of research, both at the local (Fearn 2007) and at the district or circuit level (Kautt 2002). This Element examines the casual link between legal rulings on appeal decisions in circuit courts and the subsequent sentencing decisions in the lower district courts within the circuit jurisdiction. We are unaware of any previous study of this causal question for sentencing and, more broadly, of how judicial writing style affects downstream outcomes.

In order to measure the causal impact, this Element considers sentencing lengths to be influenced by latent covariates from various political, social, and economic factors. At the core of our methodology is the use of features generated from a naturally occurring random process in our prediction task. We exploit the fact that judges of each case are randomly assigned, and we take judge characteristics as an instrumental variable (Chen et al. 2016).

2.1 Related Works on Law

Two decades ago, there were three main theories of judicial behavior – legal, attitudinal, and self-interested – the first posits that judges follow formal rules or legal philosophy (Kornhauser 1999). The latter two assume some form of bias: for example, the attitudinal model posits that judges follow political preferences (Cameron 1993) and the self-interested model posits that judges maximize their utility (Posner 1973). The distinction between legal and attitudinal is subtle: for instance, in a legal model, a judge can adhere to a strict interpretation of the Constitution, while, in an attitudinal model, the same behavior is interpreted as simply hewing to the preferences of a political party.

In recent years, the self-interested model has been reconceptualized to include identity accounts: for instance, one might gain identity utility from voting in a manner consistent with religious identity. On the other hand, self-interested decision-making can be attributed to seeking promotion. Finally, the behavioral economics revolution has entered into studies of judicial behavior. Thinking-fast judging would ascribe many of the cognitive and behavioral errors to the lack of slow, deliberate, intentional thinking.

It is a useful exercise to outline what the models of judicial behavior would predict in response to a precedent. In a legal model of judicial behavior, the judge makes decisions according to their perception of the law. Thus, a "legal" judge would follow the precedent because of the new legal rule. In an attitudinal model of judicial behavior, the precedent is only having effects on the political party's preferences. Thus, an "attitudinal" judge would follow the precedent if the political party also shifts its preferences in accordance with the precedent. In an identity account of judicial behavior, the precedent has effects if their group identity has, as a group, responded to the precedent. Thus, an "identity"-motivated judge would respond to the precedent in the same manner as their group. In a labor market model of judicial behavior, the judge makes a decision to maximize the likelihood of promotion. Following the precedent reduces the risk of reversal, which would in typical circumstances increase the likelihood of promotion. Thus, a "labor market" judge, like the "legal" judge, would also choose to follow precedent. Finally, a thinking-fast judge would make decisions according to cognitive bias or error. A precedent would influence this judge for a couple of reasons. One reason could be that the judge relies on heuristics and follows the recent precedent as a heuristic.

None of these theories easily explain a potential backlash to the precedent. Some economists have offered a unified framework for understanding how humans respond to laws and regulations. Subordinate judges in a hierarchical court system are human. Their behavioral response to a law or regulation can fit under the unified framework.

On a theoretical level, it is widely presumed that the law can affect moral values and behavior simply through its expressive power. Formal models of law (e.g., Benabou and Tirole 2011) illustrate how laws can affect the morality of particular actions. This framework examines the implications of three motivations for human behavior: intrinsic motivations (i.e., values, including ideological or identity-based motives), extrinsic motivations (i.e., material incentives, including pecuniary incentives), and social motivations (i.e., norms). Social motivations arise from the honor or stigma attributed to an individual acting outside the norm. People would like to signal their type (i.e., values) and appear moral to gain honor or avoid stigma. Legal decisions inform people about social norms. Prohibitions cause people to think that the government sees a problem. We call this an "expressive effect" when law causes what is viewed as moral to shift toward what the law values. Those who are motivated by intrinsic incentives have an easier time signaling to others as honorable. This expressive effect, however, only arises when a sufficient number of people do the stigmatized activity. When the normalizing effect exceeds the signaling effect, we call this a "backlash effect," as the law causes what is viewed as moral to shift against what the law values. When few people do the stigmatized activity, the social perception of stigmatized activities can increase substantially if the shift in beliefs causes stigmatized activities to become normalized. We use the data and methodology to test this model.

The Benabou and Tirole (2011) model encompasses many existing theories of judicial behavior when this formal framework is applied to judicial decision-making in response to legal rules. Labor market motives fall under extrinsic motivations. Legal and attitudinal motives fall under intrinsic motivations. Group identity motives fall under social motivations. Strictness or leniency in criminal justice could be stigmatized. Cognitive error is not modeled.

Our analyses are restricted to testing the causal effects of legal rulings on judicial decisions. The existing evidence on compliance of judges in lower courts to higher court rulings is scant, but some quantitative evidence exists from the USA and from Norway (Bhueller and Sigstad 2021; Chen and Frankenreiter 2021).

2.2 Related Work on Machine Learning

Methodologically, previous work by Hartford and colleagues (2017) indicates that when doing counterfactual predictions, there is a benefit from a deep instrumental variable framework, which is a two-stage deep neural network instrumental variables method. The Deep IV framework can outperform both traditional two-stage OLS and standard feed-forward networks by significantly reducing counterfactual errors.

The field of counterfactual analysis has been developing fast and has started gaining more attention from the machine learning community in recent years. Recent work from Lewis and Syrgkanis (2018) uses generative adversarial networks (GANs) and finds that GANs have a similar or better performance compared to both direct models and other forms of two-stage models. Egami and colleagues (2017) also used a related method to measure treatment effects from text and showed applicability – however, in most of their papers, the model is tested on simulated data. In contrast, the focus of this Element is on a real, complex data environment. Other papers that connect machine learning with estimating treatment effects in economics, law, and policy include Double ML (Chernozhukov et al. 2016), Causal Forest (Athey et al. 2019), and Orthogonal Random Forest (Oprescu et al. 2019).

3 Data Set

3.1 Data Set Description

This Element constructs the final data set for analysis using four raw data sets. Here, we present brief descriptions for each of them.

3.1.1 Cleaned Circuit Court Case Data

First, we have raw text records of 253,164 Circuit Court Opinions collected from 1991 to 2013, organized by year, case identification number, opinion type, and author's (judge's) last name. They contain 82,635 unique cases, 3,288 unique judge names, and 14 unique opinion types. Seventy-five percent of the cases are stated as being affirmed, and 25 percent are stated as being reversed.

3.1.2 Judge Biographical Characteristics

Second, we have demographic and background information for about 714 unique judges. The information contains a mixture of 186 numerical, textual, and categorical features, including the judges' name, age, and party affiliation, as well as their education and career backgrounds.

3.1.3 District Courts Sentencing Data

Third, we have the data set on district court sentencing information. The feature we use here is the sentencing length, which is a numerical feature ranging from 0 to 999. The number 999 represents the death sentence and hence will not be treated as a numeric value. We use interquartile range to detect outliers in the data set and thus consider data points with sentencing length greater than 152.5 as outliers. We eliminate those data from the analysis. The ones with missing values are also excluded from our analysis. The district courts' sentencing data are later joined with circuit court data by using the US state and the date of sentencing.

3.1.4 Circuit Cases Metadata

Fourth, we have a data set containing rich metadata for each circuit case, including the case ID, decision, date, three concurring judges, and case type. We use these data to filter out criminal cases that can be matched with opinion records to extract case and judge information.

Table 1 Binary decision grouping rules

Original category	Grouped as
Stay, petition, or motion granted	Reversed
Reversed (include reversed & vacated)	Reversed
Reversed and remanded (or just remanded)	Reversed
Vacated & remanded; set aside & remanded; modified & remanded	Reversed
Vacated	Reversed
Affirmed; or affirmed & petition denied	Affirmed
Petition denied or appeal dismissed	Affirmed
Affirmed in part & reversed in part; modified; Affirmed & modified	Dropped
Affirmed in part, reversed in part, and remanded	Dropped

3.2 Data Preprocessing

3.2.1 Feature Engineering

Demeaning Features: Many features in our data are potentially endogenous to court and time. For example, the number of Democrats in the court may be different each year and could have a confounding trend with outcomes. Since our data spread across twenty-three years, the changes over time might be significant. In addition, the cases are randomly assigned to judges conditional on the circuit and year. We therefore demean instruments by circuit-year to reduce the effects of confounding trends.

Target Calculation: We normalize the specified action string for the appeal decision to a binary variable, affirm or reverse. We group the seven action categories using the rules in Table 1.

We are interested in measuring the effect of an appeal decision. Therefore, we set the target variable as the change in the average sentencing length before and after an appeal decision. To do this, we measure the sentencing length changes followed by a circuit court decision using the three months before and after the decision. We subtract the average sentencing length of three months before the decision from the average sentencing length of three months after the decision. This can be seen as a first-differenced outcome by case.

3.2.2 Representing Case Text as Data

Apart from the binary appeal action (affirm or reverse), we are also interested in whether the explanation for that action – the written opinion – might have a separate impact on sentencing decisions in the district court. To take account of this, we add text features to our treatment vector. The idea is that these embedded text features would represent some writing style characteristics that capture how judges reason toward sentencing decisions. We present two methods for representing textual features. First, we construct n-gram frequencies and reduce dimensionality using principal component analysis (PCA). Second, we use document embeddings.

N-gram model with PCA: Our first approach is to represent text using n-grams. An n-gram is a word sequence of length n. The n-gram model represents a text document with a collection of n-gram that appears in the text document.

There are multiple ways to featurize the n-gram representation into a numeric vector. One of the simplest ways would be to denote the presence of an n-gram using Boolean values of 0 and 1. Other simple ways include using the counts or frequencies of the n-gram. However, these methods come with well-known issues, such as not capturing the importance of an n-gram properly. Alternatively, we use term frequency-inverse document frequency (TF-IDF) to score each n-gram. The equations for calculating TF-IDF are shown in Eqs. (1)–(3):

$$TF\text{-}IDF(t, d, D) = TF(t, d) \times IDF(t, D), \tag{1}$$

$$TF(t, d) = \frac{f_{t,d}}{\sum_{t' \in d} f_{t',d}}, \tag{2}$$

$$IDF(t, D) = log\left(\frac{N}{count(d \in D, t \in d)}\right), \tag{3}$$

where t, d, and D denote the n-gram, the document, and the corpus that contains N documents. $TF(t, d)$ measures how frequently the n-gram t occurs in current document d, and $IDF(t, D)$ measures how often the n-gram appears across all document d in the corpus D with the intuition that if an n-gram is common across many documents, then it is probably less informative about a particular document.

We convert the text documents into a TF-IDF matrix in Python and then apply PCA to reduce dimensionality and keep only the largest twenty-five principal components.

We also experiment with simple counts as scores for each n-gram. These counts featurize each document into a numeric vector. To compare the two methods, we use their resulting numeric representations of the document vectors to predict sentence length changes in an OLS regression model. We further experiment with using unigram (1-gram) or bigram (2-gram), in order to get better tradeoffs between representation power and computation cost. The result is shown in Table 2.

Table 2 Comparison of TF-IDF and count, OSL with PCA: comparing using TF-IDF score versus simple count to represent a document vector in predicting sentence length change. Used PCA to reduce the dimensionality of the document vector into twenty-five dimensions

Method	Mean Absolute Error
Count (unigram)	1.762
Count (bigram)	1.138
TF-IDF (unigram)	1.088
TF-IDF (bigram)	0.917

From the experiment, we saw that using TF-IDF is better than using simple counts. Furthermore, using bigrams gave better performance than using unigrams, which is intuitive. A further increase to 3-grams substantially increases computation burden, while the added benefit is slim. Therefore, for all the following experiments, we used bigrams with TF-IDF.

One of the limitations of this approach is the loss of information during dimensionality reduction. The information loss can be measured by the remaining explained variance of the selected principal components after PCA. We found that adding an additional principal component each time increased the explained variance by approximately 0.003, and even with 100 dimensions, the explained variance is just slightly above 10 percent of the total variance. This led us to seek a better method for representing text.

Document Embeddings: A better and more recent approach is to use document embeddings. Specifically, we used the Doc2Vec model proposed by Le and Mikolov (2014). Inspired by and similar to Word2Vec (Bengio et al. 2006; Collobert and Weston 2008; Mnih and Hinton 2008; Turian et al. 2010; Mikolov et al. 2013), Doc2Vec uses an unsupervised approach to learn feature representations from text. While the goal of Word2Vec methods is to learn representations for words, the goal of Doc2Vec is to learn representations for documents. Each document will be converted into a dense vector, where the distance between two vectors encodes the similarity between them. We trained our Doc2Vec model using a text corpus containing all cases' opinion text and used it to generate document embeddings for each case's opinion text. We used GenSim Doc2Vec implementation (Rehurek and Sojka 2010) with a context window of size 10 and generated a fixed size numeric vector of size 25 for

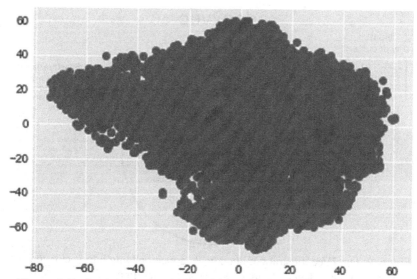

Figure 1 Projection of document embedding onto two-dimensional space. Each dot in the figure represents a case's opinion text

each case's opinion text. We used t-SNE (Van der Maaten and Hinton 2008), a tool for visualizing high-dimensional data, to project the embedding vectors onto 2-D space. The scatter plot is shown in Figure 1.

An important property of this model is that the geometric location of the embedding vector in high-dimensional space encodes predictive information for the context-specific frequencies of words in the document. Intuitively, with Doc2Vec representation, similar cases' opinion texts will be placed closer to each other in the embedding space. Le and Mikolov (2014) showed that the document vectors created with Doc2Vec outperformed other methods, including the popular bag-of-words model, for many natural language processing tasks. Figure 2 illustrates the idea of the Doc2Vec model.

3.2.3 Normalization and Splitting Data

Each circuit court has many judges, but three judges are randomly assigned to a case. We aggregate the characteristics of the three judges in each circuit court case. We normalize all columns based on mean and standard deviation. After that, we randomly split the data set into a training set, a validation set, and a test set.

The final data set has 7,388 cases as rows. Columns contain eighty-four different features for three different judges, twenty-five extracted text features from the case's opinion, a binary column indicating appeal decision (affirm/reverse), and a target column indicating sentencing length changes.

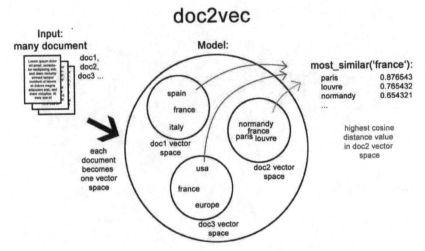

Figure 2 Doc2Vec illustration: documents are embedding into vector space where similar documents are closer to each other. Image from Gensim Doc2Vec (Rehurek and Sojka 2010)

Appendix A.2 contains a detailed description of the data set and features. The descriptive statistics are based on values after demeaning and before normalization.

4 Empirical Model

The statistical approach is mainly based on the two-stage Deep IV framework proposed by Hartford and colleagues (2017), which is a high-dimensional generalization of the reduced form causal analysis approach described by Angrist and colleagues (1996).

The Deep IV framework assumes the structural form shown in Eqs. (4) and (5) and defines the counterfactual prediction function as Eq. (6). The graphical model is illustrated in Figure 3.

$$y = G(w,x) + e, \tag{4}$$

$$w = f(x,z,e), \tag{5}$$

$$h(w,x) := G(w,x) + E[e|x], \tag{6}$$

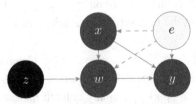

Figure 3 Model illustration. Adapted from Hartford and colleagues (2017)

where y, w, x, z, and e are the target variable, the treatment variable, observed covariates, instruments, and the error term, respectively, that contain unobserved variables. The model further assumes $E[e] = 0$, and $E[e|x, w] \neq 0$, $E[we|x] \neq 0$. With the use of instrumental variable z that satisfies the relevance assumption, exclusion assumption, and unconfounded instrument assumption, the counterfactual analysis we are interested in would be $h(w_1, x) - h(w_0, x)$, where w_0 is the base treatment, w_1 is the target treatment, and $h(w, x)$ is the solution to the inverse problem (8). Interested readers should refer to Hartford and colleagues (2017) for more details.

$$E[y|x, z] = E[G(w, x)|x, z] + E[e|x], \tag{7}$$

$$= \int h(w, x) dF[w|x, z]. \tag{8}$$

In this Element, the treatment variable (w) contains the appeal decision and accompanying opinion text features of the US Circuit Court. Our outcome (y) is the sentencing length change (from three months before to three months after) in the corresponding district courts. The instrumental variable (z) is the randomly assigned circuit judge characteristic. The variable (x) contains possible covariates of the circuit case, such as detailed topic. The confounder (e) is correlated with the treatment variable (w) and the outcome (y) but not with the instruments (z).

To measure the effect of criminal appeal decisions in circuit courts on the changes in sentencing decisions of district courts, we are going to carry out three main prediction tasks.

First, Deep OLS involves training $F(y|w)$. We train a model to predict the district court sentencing length changes (y) using the appeal decision and opinion text features (w).

Second, what we call "Deep Reduced Form," which involves training $F(y|z)$. We train a model to predict district court sentencing length changes (y) from the judges' characteristics (z).

Third, we have the "Deep IV" or "Deep 2SLS" approach. This is a machine learning implementation of the two-stage Deep IV framework proposed by Hartford and colleagues (2017). In the first stage, we will be training $F(w|z)$ and predict the circuit court appeal decisions and opinions (w) using judge characteristics (z). There are twenty-six different target variables, and we form a prediction $\hat{w}$ and measure the R^2 for each. In the second stage, we are predicting y by learning the function $G(y|\hat{w})$. That is, we use the outcome of the circuit court appeal decisions and text features from the first stage model to predict the sentencing length changes.

Table 3 Model comparison: predicting sentencing length changes with only text features from each case's opinion text. Four popular machine learning models are used in the comparison. The performances are measured using mean squared error and mean absolute error

Model	MSE	Mean Absolute Error
Random forest	1.55	0.90
Decision tree	2.53	1.19
SVM	1.48	0.87
Gradient boosting	1.44	0.86

We compare the models on performance in prediction tasks and statistical tests. For predictability, we measure the out-of-sample mean squared error and R^2. The formula for computing R^2 is shown in Eq. (9), where $\hat{y}_i$ is the predicted sentence length change.

$$R^2 = 1 - \frac{\sum_i (y_i - \hat{y}_i)^2}{\sum_i (y_i - \bar{y})^2}. \tag{9}$$

5 Results

5.1 Deep OLS

For the Deep OLS model, we use the extracted text features of the circuit court case, which encodes the judge's writing style, and circuit court decision (affirm/reverse) to directly predict district court sentencing length change y. We experimented with both the n-gram model with the PCA approach and the document embedding approach.

We also experimented with different algorithms to see the predictive power of the text features. Using only the text features, we compared different regression models: decision tree regressor (Quinlan 1986), support vector regressor (Cortes and Vapnik 1995), gradient boosting regressor (Friedman 2001), and random forest regressor (Liaw and Wiener 2002). Results are given in Table 3.

Among the compared models, gradient boosting regressor performs the best. We will later compare gradient boosting regressor with a neural network.

Next, we included the circuit court appeal decision (reverse/affirm) as a feature. We compared a two-layer neural network with gradient boosting regressor. We implement the network in pytorch (Paszke et al. 2019). We applied dropout (Srivastava et al. 2014) and batch normalization (Ioffe and Szegedy 2015) to avoid overfitting and facilitate training. In machine learning, hyperparameters are those parameters that define the model architecture and control the learning process. We didn't perform extensive hyperparameter searches on the neural network due to its high computation cost. We performed a grid search on the gradient boosting regressor to select the best hyperparameters within the search space using the validation set. The n-gram model with the PCA approach gave us a mean squared error of 0.82 and a mean absolute error of 0.72 on the test set for neural network and a mean squared error of 0.62 and a mean absolute error of 0.64 for gradient boosting regressor. For this particular data set and task, the gradient boosting regressor performed slightly better than our neural network. We will discuss some possible reasons in Section 5.4.

For the document embedding approaches, the best performance is achieved using gradient boosting regressor with Doc2Vec text representations (Le and Mikolov 2014); the mean square error is 0.65. We also experimented with another more recent document embedding method proposed by Arora and colleagues (2017) and found that it did not achieve better performance than Doc2Vec for our data set and task.

5.2 Deep Reduced Form

The Deep Reduced Form analysis is to predict district court sentencing length y from the judges' characteristics z by training $F(y|z)$. We monitor the change of average sentencing length from three months before the circuit court decision to three months after the circuit court decision from the same circuit area demeaned by circuit-year.

We tried a range of models. We tried to fit neural network, linear regression, ridge regression, lasso regression, gradient boosting regressor, and random forest regressor. We used mean squared error to measure model performances.

Among these models, random forest regressor performs the best. The hyper parameter is chosen according to validation performance. The best mean squared error is 0.49. The scatter plot of true and predicted values is given in Figure 4. The instruments have clear predictive power, as the predicted value is increasing with the real value of the target. The R^2 of our prediction is 0.094.

Next, we plot the feature importance as reported from the random forest. Feature importance shows for a particular model and the task at hand how much a feature affects the final prediction. We report this both with and without the demeaning step in Figures 5 and 6 (a description of the feature name can be seen in Appendix A.2). We see that demeaning makes a big difference in terms of feature importance. Without demeaning, the most important features are mainly about the number of Republicans and Democrats, as well as the judges' own party. After demeaning, the most important features include whether a judge is a Solicitor-General, the age of the judge, and the number of Republicans in the Senate at the year of appointment. This demonstrates the importance of

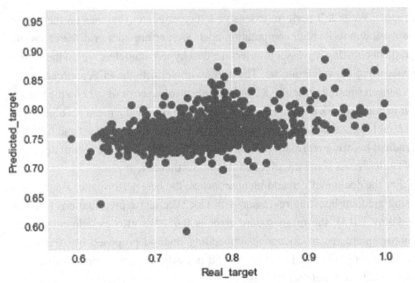

Figure 4 Reduced Form Model predicted values versus real target: plotting the real sentence length change on *x*-axis and predicted sentence length change on *y*-axis. Each dot represents a case

potential confounders for the OLS estimates. Binscatter plots[1] of two important demeaned features are also presented in Figures 7 and 8.

The random forest feature importance ranking does not tell the direction of the effect of the predictors. To see the direction of the effects, we fit a linear regression separately for each of the top ten important instruments in the reduced form. These coefficients are reported in Table 4. We can see that number of Republicans in the Senate (at the time of appointment) increases sentence lengths and older judges (those born in the 1910s) decrease sentence lengths.

5.3 Deep2SLS

This section reports the results from a Deep2SLS approach for the impact of affirm/reverse on sentence lengths. We will predict circuit court appeal decision (affirm/reverse) and the text features (twenty-five dimensions numeric values) in the first stage. We will then use the first-stage predictions to measure the treatment effect in the second stage.

---

[1] Binscatter plot is an effective way of visualizing the relationship between two variables when the number of data points is too crowded to be shown in standard scatter plots (Stepner 2014). It is created by grouping *x*-axis variables into equal-sized bins, drawing the scatter plot using the mean of the *x*- and *y*-axes variable with each bin, and drawing a population regression line over the data.

Table 4 Reduced Form feature importance and regression coefficient: showing ten important features according to feature importance by random forest regressor. Each of these feature is then fit individually in linear regressor to obtain the coefficient

Features	Importance	Coefficient	Standard error
Solicitor-General	0.052	−0.175	0.113
Born in 1910s	0.042	−0.061	0.031
Number of members of other political parties	0.034	0.049	0.023
Justice Department	0.031	0.035	0.030
Number of Republicans in the Senate	0.028	0.001	0.002
Age at time of commission	0.028	−0.001	0.002
Full-time law professor	0.026	−0.002	0.020
Deputy or assistant district/ county/city attorney	0.025	−0.016	0.034
Born in 1940s	0.024	0.0056	0.019
JD obtained in public school	0.023	−0.010	0.017

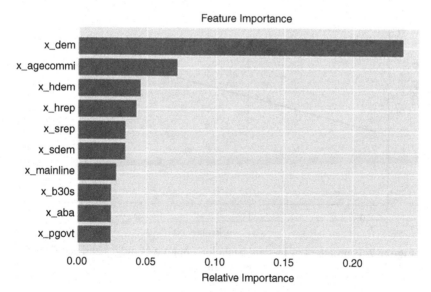

Figure 5 Reduced Form feature importance before demeaning

5.3.1 First Stage

In the first stage, we predict circuit court appeal decision (affirm/reverse) and text features using judge characteristics. We have eighty-four features for each

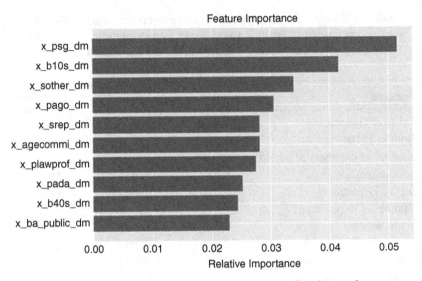

Figure 6 Reduced Form feature importance after demeaning

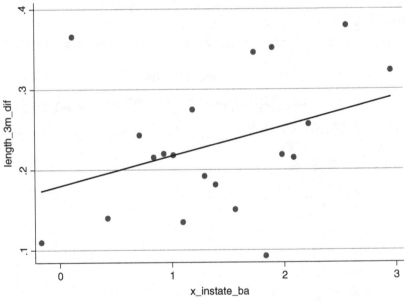

Figure 7 Binscatters of in-state bachelor's degree of judges and sentencing length change

person. We sum the three values up based on each feature for the classification task.

For circuit court appeal decision, we experimented with several different classification models, including logistic regression (Cox 1958), gradient boosting (Friedman 2001), and random forest (Liaw and Wiener 2002). Area under

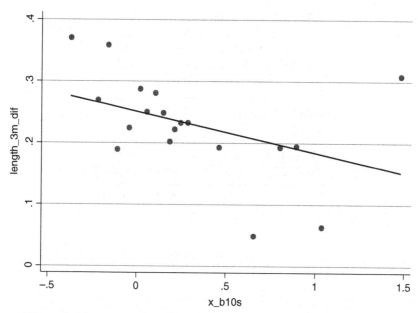

Figure 8 Binscatters of judges born in the 1910s and sentencing length change

the ROC[2] Curve (AUC) was used as the evaluation metric for this task. The best AUC score is 0.86 on validation set, achieved by random forest classifier with *maxdepth* = 6 and *numtrees* = 120. The ROC curve and confusion matrix[3] are reported in Figure 9 and Table 5. The F1 score[4] of the categorical prediction is 0.18. The model's other performance statistics are MSE = .145, RMS = .38, LogLoss = .46, and Gini = .204.

The feature importance for predicting affirm/reverse decision are shown in Figures 10 and 11 (description of the feature name can be seen in Appendix A.2). The bar plots show the top ten important features derived by Random Forest model. We can see that the feature ranking does not change nearly as much as it did in the reduced form. They are quite similar. Both the reduced form and first stage rely on random assignment. It could be coincidental that demeaning matters more in reduced form. The causal interpretation rests on demeaning. The first stage results being more similar with and without demeaning may be because judges have a much more direct effect on their own decisions

---

[2] A ROC is created by plotting the true positive rate against the false positive rate at various thresholds, thus showing the trade-off between true positive rate and false positive rate for the given classifier.

[3] A confusion matrix is a technique for summarizing the performance of a classification algorithm; it shows different combinations of the predicted and actual values.

[4] F1 score is defined as the harmonic mean of precision and recall.

Table 5 Confusion matrix: first stage prediction of affirm/reverse. Showing the actual circuit court appeal decision by rows and the predicted circuit court appeal decision by columns

Prediction: Actual:	Affirmed	Reversed	Error
Affirmed	470	419	0.471
Reversed	73	123	0.372
Total	543	542	0.453

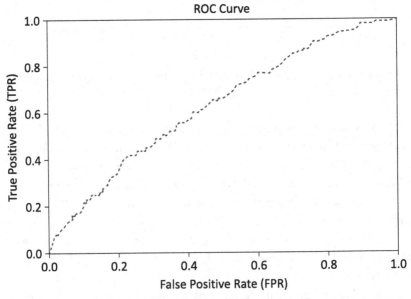

Figure 9 ROC curve: first stage prediction of affirm/reverse

(affirm/reverse) than they do on the decisions of the district court judges in their jurisdictions.

Using feature importance to guide our exploration, we further built a logistic regression model on several selected features of interest to see whether each of them is positively or negatively correlated with the target variable. These coefficients are reported in Table 6. We see that Democrat judges and Jewish judges are more likely to reverse lower-court decisions. These are pro-defendant, liberal decisions. In turn, Catholics tend to affirm lower-court decisions. This means they are more conservative in this area.

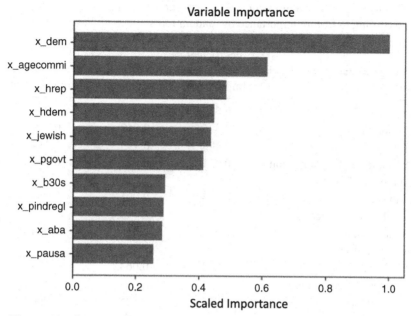

Figure 10 First stage feature importance in predicting circuit court decision (before demeaning)

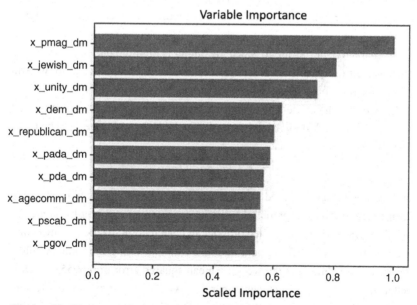

Figure 11 First stage feature importance in predicting circuit court decision (after demeaning)

For text features, we used the document embedding of twenty-five dimensions we generated from Doc2Vec (Le and Mikolov 2014) as our target, and

Table 6 First stage regression coefficient: showing ten important features according to feature importance by random forest. Each of these feature is then fit individually in logisitc regression to obtain the coefficient.

Variable	Importance	Coefficient	Standard error
Jewish	0.037	−0.036	0.007
Democrat	0.025	−0.049	0.059
Born in 1950s	0.023	0.193	0.114
Age at time of Commission	0.023	0.026	0.004
Number of Republicans in the House	0.015	0.005	0.006
Number of Democrats in the Senate	0.015	−0.053	0.064
American Bar Association Rating	0.013	−0.064	0.035
Number of Democrats in the House	0.013	0.025	0.006
Number of Republicans in the Senate	0.013	0.056	0.063
Catholic	0.012	0.122	0.057

judge characteristics as input. Since the output is high-dimensional, we fit one regressor for every individual text feature dimension. In this scenario, we still choose random forest as the regression model.

After fitting the models, we calculate the R^2 for every regressor on the test set. The R^2 for each dimension is reported in Table 7 and Figure 12. The mean R^2 is 0.03.

5.3.2 Second Stage

In the second stage, we used as input the output of first stage and used a two-layer neural network to predict the district court sentencing length change. As in DeepOLS section, we applied dropout and batch normalization to the neural network to avoid overfitting and facilitate training. Using the same architecture as in DeepOLS section, we get a mean squared error of 0.6955, which is better than the result we get using neural networks for all types of text feature representations in the DeepOLS section. This demonstrates the applicability of deep instrumental variables to legal data. Although the neural network here still performs a little worse than Gradient Boosting Regressor in the DeepOLS section, we argue that this might be mainly caused by the small size of our data. A common wisdom is that neural networks usually outperform traditional

Table 7 First stage R^2 for document embedding: using judge characteristics to predict document embedding. Showing the R^2 for each dimension of the document embedding when fitting to the random forest regressor

Text feature	1	2	3	4	5	6	7	8	9	10
R^2	0.023	0.057	−0.003	0.068	0.031	−0.009	0.035	−0.002	−0.008	0.015
Text feature	11	12	13	14	15	16	17	18	19	20
R^2	−0.015	0.025	0.036	0.004	0.007	−0.009	0.059	0.007	0.057	0.008
Text feature	21	22	23	24	25					
R^2	0.055	0.013	0.016	0.005	0.034					

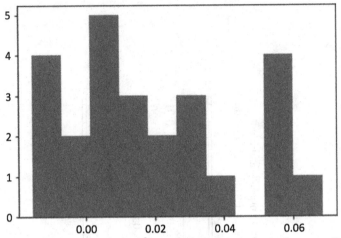

Figure 12 Distribution of R^2. Using judge characteristics to predict document embedding

machine learning algorithms as the data set becomes larger. We hypothesize that with a larger data set we can build deeper neural networks and achieve better performance.

To see the effect of circuit court appeal decisions (affirm/reverse) on district court sentencing, we used only the predicted (affirm/reverse) decision as predictor to predict sentencing length change y. In Table 8, we also group the sentencing length changes by the predicted (affirm/reverse) as well as the actual (affirm/reverse) decision and compare the mean and variance. Tables 8 and 9 show the details of various statistics.

By fitting the linear regression to predict sentencing length from predicted binary decision, setting Affirmed to 1 and Reversed to 0, we get the 2SLS coefficient of Affirm decision to be −0.0739 and standard error 0.027. The interpretation is that affirming the lower court decision (i.e., being harsh on criminal defendants) leads to a weak decrease in sentence lengths. The result seems counterintuitive.

Thus, we further investigated this issue by examining the effect of circuit court decision on district court sentencing length deviation from sentencing guidelines (more precisely, a percentile relative to the recommended sentence minimum and maximum). For a case i, we compute its percentile as follows:

$$\text{percentile}_i = (\text{sentence-length}_i - \text{glmin}_i)/(\text{glmax}_i - \text{glmin}_i) \qquad (10)$$

To measure the impacts on the percentile relative to sentencing guidelines, we subtract the average percentile of three months before the decision from the average percentile of three months after the decision. Using this outcome

Table 8 Differences in sentence length (month) by affirm/reverse decision of circuit case: showing various statistics for the difference in sentence length by the appeals decision of circuit court. The statistics used are the count (number of cases), mean, standard deviation, 25 percentile, 50 percentile, 75 percentile, minimum and maximum

Real target	Count	Mean	Std	Min	25%	50%	75%	Max
Reversed	1300.0	0.275407	1.260136	−16.056524	−0.432869	0.220238	0.877178	5.432741
Affirmed	6088.0	0.228661	1.139971	−3.356841	−0.460344	0.198438	0.850322	5.432741

Table 9 Differences in sentence length (month) by predicted affirm/reverse decision of circuit case: showing various statistics for the difference in predicted sentence length by the appeals decision of circuit court. The statistics used are the count (number of cases), mean, standard deviation, 25 percentile, 50 percentile, 75 percentile, minimum and maximum

Prediction	Count	Mean	Std	Min	25%	50%	75%	Max
Reversed	3020.0	0.280601	1.20669	−16.056524	−0.421325	0.257049	0.898100	5.432741
Affirmed	4368.0	0.206663	1.12933	−3.356841	−0.465167	0.172272	0.823898	5.432741

variable, we find that the coefficient of Affirm decision to sentencing deviation is 0.00758, and standard error is 0.003. Since the recommended sentence length is based on the charges brought forward by the prosecutor, the statistically significant positive effects on percentile relative to sentencing guidelines and insignificant negative effects on actual sentence lengths is likely due to the interplay between prosecutors and judges.

When a circuit judge issues a harsh decision (affirming the lower court ruling), prosecutors backlash by issuing more lenient charges. In the meantime, district judges are largely obeying the circuit rulings, resulting in a positive effect. It is an empirical question whether the prosecutor becomes harsher or more lenient after a judicial ruling. If judicial rulings are more salient to prosecutors when they go in the opposite direction of a prosecutor's preferences, the prosecutor may behave in a strategic manner to undermine that judicial ruling.

5.3.3 Correspondence to Theoretical Models

District judges' compliance with legal precedent would be consistent with the legal model and the labor market model, and be less easily explained by the attitudinal or identity model. A "legal" judge would follow the precedent because of the new legal rule. A "labor market" judge, like the "legal" judge, would also choose to follow precedent. However, an "attitudinal" judge would follow the precedent if the political party also shifts their preferences in accordance to the precedent. Likewise, an "identity"-motivated judge would follow the precedent if their group chooses to shift preferences with the precedent. It is also possible that a "thinking-fast" judge follows precedent because it is a heuristic. Additional data, like measures of judicial attention or brain activation, would be needed. A "labor market" judge is potentially distinguished from a "legal" judge by the group audience (is it near elections, is the judge under consideration for promotion, etc.).

Prosecutorial backlash would not be explained by the legal model. The attitudinal or identity-model may play a role. Data would be needed on the behavioral response in the preferences of the party and the group identity and also the group identity of the prosecutor. A labor market model may explain this behavior. Data would be needed to correlate the backlash with future promotion. To attribute the backlash to thinking fast, data would be needed on the source of behavioral bias. Finally, backlashing to a legal rule may be attributable to the behavior being less stigmatized. Data would be needed to measure a prosecutor's beliefs about the norms and how these beliefs are affected by the precedent.

5.4 Discussion

Our experiments suggest that the neural network benefits from using a two-stage model compared to direct DeepOLS approach, because after controlling for the same model architecture and feature representation method, the two-stage approach achieves lower mean squared error and higher R^2. This is evidence that the inclusion of instrumental variables is helping with measuring causal effects and reducing counterfactual errors during prediction.

After reducing latent variable variations using two-stage IV methods, we believe the prediction of sentencing length change from appeal decision and opinion text is causal. We interpret our results as suggesting that prosecutors are backlashing, while judges are complying to circuit court decisions. Using the IV framework, we also believe this result is causal.

Our experimentation with models on different stages shows that ensemble methods generally provide best results in almost all model selections, including linear regression with kernel and neural networks. Using same data partition to compare, they generally have higher R^2 scores and lower mean square error. This is interesting as neural networks are generally more commonly used among high-dimensional features. We suspect that this may be due to our relatively small data set.

6 On the Practical Use of Deep IV for Law and Economics

Legal scholars and judges have long made and justified their arguments about laws and regulations with theories about the effects of these legal rules. The situation resembles the field of medicine a century ago: prior to the advent of clinical trials, there were only theories without rigorous causal evidence. A growing body of empirical research demonstrates that causal inference is possible when cases are randomly assigned to judges. Randomizing cases to judges with different decision-making tendencies generates the inference on the long-run causal impacts of those decisions. This raises the possibility of a law platform that has four parts: first, automatically identifying the nearest previous cases when a case appears; second, fast-decision classification of the prior cases' directionalities; third, the use of document embeddings for low-dimensional representation of legal dicta and reasoning; fourth, the use of judge embeddings based on the history of their writings and citations to predict their verdicts on cases. The latter can be used to support judges in estimating the potential impacts of their rulings on downstream economic outcomes.

Formally, given treatment variables (law) w, instrument variables (judge characteristics) z, target variables (outcomes) y, and covariates x, the Deep IV model involves two main steps. First, a model of choice F is trained to predict the treatment variable w using the instrument z and covariates x. Then, the predicted treatments, $\hat{w}$, instead of the true treatments, w, are used together with covariates X to predict the target variable y using another model of choice G. Deep IV model is a method for performing counterfactual analysis. The basic idea behind the model is to remove the effect from unobserved confounders using instrument variables so as to estimate the true treatment effect.

To use the Deep IV model in practice, one can implement the models themselves with the proper graphical model as discussed in Section 4. The key requirement is to identify proper instruments z that only affect the target y through the treatments w. In this Element, we implemented the models by using the randomly assigned circuit judge characteristics as instruments and assume that the judge characteristics only affect the sentencing through the treatments.

Alternatively, one can also use the publicly available Deep IV implementation released as part of the EconML toolkit[5] (Microsoft Research 2019). The EconML toolkit is a python package dedicated for estimating treatment effect via machine learning models. In their Deep IV implementation, the model $F(w|z,x)$ is chosen to be a mixture density network (Bishop 2006).

The Deep IV module in the EconML toolkit allows the user to either predict the outcomes y_i, given treatment assignment w_i and covariates x_i, or directly estimate the treatment effect, which is calculated as the difference in outcomes based on two treatment points (i.e., the base treatment and the target treatment). We find that it can actually be extended to a suite of higher dimensional treatments and instruments. In this Element, we have a high-dimensional treatment vector. We can use the 5th percentile values of each dimension in the document embedding vector, together with the affirm decision as a base treatment. Additionally, we use the 95th percentile values of each dimension in the document embedding vector, together with the reverse decision as the target treatment.

There are several challenges when applying Deep IV to real-world problems. Next, we discuss some common challenges and bring forth some suggestions on how to view and address them.

Sensitivity to hyperparameters and network architecture. Similar to many other machine learning methods, the Deep IV method is sensitive to hyperparameter settings. In the EconML Deep IV module, for example, the first stage network uses the mixture density model. The hyperparameter K, which controls the number of mixture components used, is usually an important hyperparameter

---

[5] https://github.com/microsoft/EconML.

that can have strong influence on final performance. Generally speaking, with larger K, the model has larger capacity and is able to fit more flexible models, but requires larger data set. The network architecture (e.g., the number of layers and the number of neurons in each layer) can also play an important role. Again, a larger model usually requires more data. Better computing may address this issue. The same arguments also apply when one tries to implement the two-stage model themselves.

Difficulty in hyperparameter selection. In contrast to many machine learning models where the goal is to make good prediction on new data, counterfactual analyses ask the "What-if" question. This poses a unique challenge, since we do not have the ground truth. Without the ground truth, we cannot use the standard hyperparameter selection approach, where we use a validation set that are assumed to be from the same data distribution as the train set and test set, and use the model performance on the validation set to select hyperparameters.

This problem is not unique to Deep IV and hence also concerns other counterfactual analysis methods. These methods are usually developed using synthetic data, where the researchers define the data-generating process, and thus know the true treatment effect. A method is successful if it recovers the true treatment effect. In contrast, we are applying the counterfactual analysis to real-world data that come from a complicated data-generating process where we do not know the true treatment effect, making hyperparameter selection a challenging task.

A workaround would be to still use the standard validation set and to use the validation loss to select hyperparameters, hoping that the validation loss correctly reflects the actual performance in counterfactual analysis.

Randomness. Randomness in the estimation might be another practical concern. To be specific, even with same data split, hyperparameters and network architecture, there could still be (at times substantial) variation between different runs of the model. This is somewhat expected given that Deep IV usually utilizes neural networks as the model of choice. Common sources of the randomness include random initialization of the network weights, randomness caused by optimization algorithms like stochastic gradient descent, and randomness caused by the use of regularization methods like dropout (Srivastava et al. 2014).

One way to address this issue is to set a random seed at the beginning. Another common practice within the machine learning community would be to average the results across multiple runs to get a more reliable estimate of the true treatment effect.

However, depending on the actual problem and data set, if the variation is too large, this might also indicate issues such as not having enough data, not choosing the suitable architecture for the problem, or not satisfying some of Deep IV's assumptions.

Overall, we are excited about fast development in counterfactual analysis with machine learning. However, we would like to emphasize that these models should be used with caution and in conjunction with theories in economics and law, while the results should be interpreted from the context of policy and theory.

7 Limitations from a Computer Science Perspective

Social science prediction is challenging, and judicial decisions are no exception. The future availability of better modeling methods may improve on the limitations of our analysis and limited data. Most of our predictions have a low R^2, which generally indicates a poor fit for prediction purposes. Although our data on all cases are substantial, we still argue that the aforementioned problem might be largely caused by the small size of the available data. The number of criminal cases that have both opinion data and all judges' characteristics is not very large. Furthermore, the district sentencing data only range from 1991 to 2013, which is also limiting our selection. The final data set we use for modeling contains only 7,388 data points, which could be too small given this particularly challenging problem. Accordingly, we think the predictability of models is hugely affected by this, in part explaining our R^2 and F1 score results.

When predicting the circuit court appeal decision, our target variable (appeal decision) is imbalanced and our F1 score unsatisfying. To deal with this issue, we could try to down-sample or up-sample our data so as to make the model more robust. In our case, however, this might make our data set even smaller.

When representing data, we also didn't substantially explore all possible dimension space. Trying out a different size of text feature representation may yield better modeling results.

Another limitation is that, due to the availability of data, we did not consider latent covariates in the two-stage model, which Hartford and colleagues (2017) included. We think that including covariates in the models will also help with increasing the overall predictability of models.

8 Limitations from an Economics Perspective

Judge leniency designs have become one of the most popular instrumental variables in applied econometrics. The design first gained attention in studies of criminal sentencing, but has now been used to study the effects of disability insurance, pre-trial detention, patent protection, debt relief, hospital choice, and business acceleration. Our setting of appellate outcomes is similar. Limitations in these settings include examining closely the actual assignment mechanism. Do judges serve in certain time periods? We have controlled for the unit of randomization with circuit X month fixed effects, which is the best we can do without the actual computer record of who was available to be assigned for any given case. Is randomization at the case level or in batches? This determines whether it is an individual or clustered random assignment. To the best of our knowledge, cases are assigned individually. Access to the computer that generates the random assignment would be necessary to know.

Another caveat is the exclusion restriction. Judges may say things in court that can change defendants' beliefs and attitudes and they may impose conditions on defendants apart from sentence length. The exclusion seems easier to justify when there's no interaction between the decision-maker and the case decision. Yet another concern arises. Is the decision multidimensional? The research on multivalued simultaneous treatments is nascent. The best research to date suggests using Lasso to pool and select among treatments. Investigating this in detail is beyond the scope of this Element.

A final oft-raised concern with instrumental variables is the assumption of monotonicity, which means an instrumental variable estimator yields LATE – the impact for people whose status is affected by the stricter or lenient judge. Monotonicity assumes judges are uniformly more or less lenient. An individual punished by a lenient judge would also be punished by a strict judge. This assumption can become trickier in judicial panels. This makes the IV estimator harder to interpret beyond being the weighted average of some treatment effects.

A last concern is statistical power. How much difference does a judge make? If judges have strong habits and these habits affect litigant outcomes, the easier it is to use the methods proposed here.

9 Potential Future Work

This Element provides experiments concerning causal analyses of criminal sentencing. Future work may include expanding data to a larger time range, adding historical features of judges' writing style, including covariates in the two-stage model, and further fine-tuning of all models. We hope this work offers some insights and results for using two-stage Deep IV models in causal investigations of law and judges' decision-making.

Large data sets of legal judgments exist beyond the US setting. For instance, India's Kanoon legal search engine has eighty-four million cases since before the Partition. Brazil has fourteen million labor cases and twenty-five million federal cases alone in one legal search engine. More broadly, there are many settings where law and economics can benefit from the method. Legal scholars and judges have long made arguments about laws and regulations and justified their arguments with theories about the effects of these legal rules. This situation resembles the field of medicine a century ago: prior to the advent of clinical trials, there were only theories without rigorous causal evidence. A growing body of empirical research now demonstrates that causal inference is possible when cases are randomly assigned to judges in any domain. Randomizing cases to judges with different decision-making tendencies generates the inference on the long-run causal impacts of those decisions. The larger application of this research is toward developing a law platform that has four parts: first, automatically identify the nearest previous cases when a case appears; second, fast-decision classification of the prior cases' directionalities; third, use document embeddings for low-dimensional representation of legal dicta and reasoning; fourth, use judge embeddings based on the history of their writings and citations to predict their verdicts on cases. This can be used to support judges in estimating the potential impacts of their rulings on downstream outcomes.

Appendix

A.1 Distribution of Predicted Sentence Length Change

As an additional comparison, we plotted the distribution of the predicted sentence length change $\hat{y}$ for the main specifications using a neural network. These are reported in Figures A1 through A3. We can see that the distribution is quite different across the specifications. It shows that there is some omitted variable bias in the OLS specification, which has been corrected in the 2SLS specification.

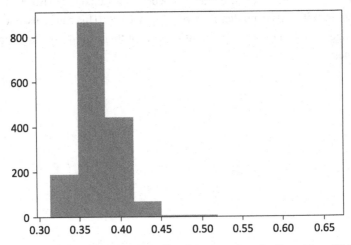

Figure A1 Distribution of predicted target using doc2vec DeepOLS

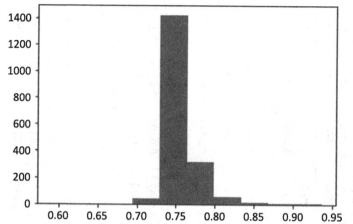

Figure A2 Distribution of predicted target using Deep Reduced Form

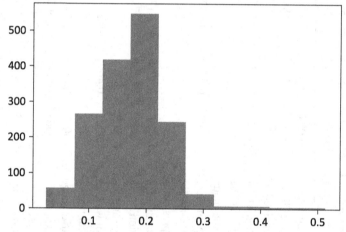

Figure A3 Distribution of predicted target using doc2vec Deep2sls

A.2 Detailed Description of the Data Set and Features

Table A1 Judge characteristics: we aggregate the characteristics of the three judges in each circuit court case, and demean by circuit year

Feature name	Description	Mean	Std	Min	25%	50%	75%	Max
x_dem_dm	Is democrat	-0.009	0.7718	-2.0541	-0.5763	-0.0496	0.6	2.5806
x_republican_dm	Is replublican	0.009	0.7718	-2.5806	-0.6	0.0496	0.5763	2.0541
x_instate_ba_dm	Whether B.A. received in same state as appointment	0.0006	0.7849	-2.1857	-0.5	-0.0227	0.5513	2.0702
x_elev_dm	If judge was elevated from the district court president who made the district bench appointment	-0.0027	0.7541	-1.9773	-0.5067	-0.0473	0.5648	2.3578
x_unity_dm	Whether government (Congress and president) was unified or divided	-0.0058	0.7259	-1.5128	-0.5263	-0.0496	0.4746	2.5806
x_aba_dm	American Bar Association rating	0.0077	1.0578	-3.2715	-0.7326	0.0642	0.6543	5.369
x_crossa_dm	Whether the judge and the appointing president were of the same or different political parties	-0.0001	0.4004	-0.8529	-0.2267	-0.1266	0	2.5185
x_pfedjdge_dm	If is federal district judge	-0.0021	0.7531	-2.2807	-0.507	0	0.5294	2.6341
x_pindreg1_dm	If have other federal experience	0.0064	0.6564	-1.5034	-0.4722	-0.093	0.4833	2.2899
x_plawprof_dm	Full-time law professor	-0.0003	0.6657	-2.0727	-0.5135	-0.1429	0.4652	2.5811
x_pscab_dm	Sub-cabinet secretary	0.0015	0.3403	-1.3333	-0.138	-0.0167	0	1.9737
x_pcab_dm	Sub-cabinet secretary	0	0.034	-0.087	0	0	0	0.9292

x_pusa_dm	US Attorney	0.0034	0.3771	-0.8913	-0.22	-0.0481	0	2.25
x_pssenate_dm	State senate	0.0006	0.2095	-0.3793	-0.0476	0	0	1.7769
x_paag_dm	Sub-cabinet secretary, Department of Justice	-0.0002	0.2971	-1.2667	-0.0927	-0.01	0	1.9073
x_psp_dm	Special prosecutor	0.0011	0.0876	-0.1704	0	0	0	0.9628
x_pslc_dm	State lower court judge	0.0011	0.6349	-1.44	-0.5435	-0.087	0.3611	2.4762
x_pssc_dm	State lower court judge	0.0009	0.4581	-0.7324	-0.3155	-0.156	0.2676	2.4561
x_pshouse_dm	State house	0.0002	0.2875	-0.561	-0.1233	-0.0357	0	1.9057
x_psg_dm	Solicitor-General	-0.0003	0.1086	-0.3684	0	0	0	0.9925
x_psgo_dm	Solicitor-General's office	-0.0015	0.2445	-0.873	-0.0198	0	0	2.2069
x_psenate_dm	US Senate	-0.0004	0.0875	-0.3684	0	0	0	0.9545
x_psatty_dm	Atate attorney	0.007	0.5997	-1.3684	-0.4667	-0.2131	0.4649	2.6408
x_pprivate_dm	Private practice	-0.0045	0.3957	-2.5877	0	0.0374	0.1842	1
x_pmayor_dm	Mayor	-0.0004	0.2065	-0.4412	-0.0714	0	0	0.9912
x_ploct_dm	Local/municipal court judge	0.0002	0.3733	-0.5455	-0.2111	-0.0878	0	1.9122
x_phouse_dm	US House of Representatives	-0.0012	0.182	-0.3333	-0.0253	0	0	0.9912
x_pgov_dm	Governor	-0.0008	0.1337	-0.3	-0.0097	0	0	0.9912
x_pda_dm	District/County/City Attorney	0.002	0.3132	-0.7273	-0.0642	0	0	1.9358
x_pcc_dm	Congressional counsel	-0.0004	0.2513	-0.6875	-0.0826	0	0	1.6889
x_pccoun_dm	City council	-0.0005	0.1949	-0.4138	-0.0106	0	0	1.8582
x_pausa_dm	Assistant US Attorney	0.0013	0.4239	-1.3571	-0.2727	-0.0968	0	2.4091

Table A1 *(Continued.)*

Feature name	Description	Mean	Std	Min	25%	50%	75%	Max
x_pada_dm	Deputy or assistant district/county/city attorney	0.0032	0.4343	−1.3333	−0.2027	−0.0283	0	2.7368
x_pgovt_dm	Any governmental experience	−0.0047	0.6331	−2.3014	−0.2844	0	0.3333	1.7143
x_llm_sjd_dm	Master of Laws (LL.M.) and Doctor of Juridical Science (S.J.D.)?	0.0018	0.4813	−1.1053	−0.2667	−0.0909	0.2358	2.3372
x_protestant_dm	Protestant	0.0006	0.7436	−2.2553	−0.52	0.004	0.5333	2.5405
x_evangelical_dm	Evangelical	0.002	0.4768	−0.8	−0.2533	−0.0912	0.2562	2.449
x_mainline_dm	Mainline Protestants	−0.0016	0.727	−2.1818	−0.5217	0.0571	0.5057	2.5405
x_noreligion_dm	No religion	−0.0012	0.2572	−0.4123	−0.119	0	0	1.7828
x_catholic_dm	Catholic	−0.0015	0.6927	−1.8421	−0.6395	0.0678	0.3636	2.6061
x_jewish_dm	Jewish	0.0003	0.5307	−1.5901	−0.2734	−0.0997	0.2895	2.8391
x_black_dm	Black	0.0001	0.3532	−0.8235	−0.2049	−0.0693	0	1.8182
x_nonwhite_dm	Non-White	0	0.4781	−0.8235	−0.3165	−0.1739	0.4286	2.5294
x_female_dm	Female	−0.0017	0.5269	−1.12	−0.3883	−0.1759	0.4571	2.6429
x_jd_public_dm	BA obtained in public school	0.0085	0.7718	−2.1429	−0.5149	−0.0164	0.4921	2.3539
x_ba_public_dm	JD obtained in public school	−0.0038	0.7435	−2.0435	−0.4474	−0.0256	0.5072	2.6957
x_b10s_dm	Age information	−0.0018	0.4596	−1.2	−0.3226	−0.1009	0.1667	2.157
x_b20s_dm	Age information	−0.0064	0.6697	−1.55	−0.5065	−0.1522	0.45	2.6667
x_b30s_dm	Age information	0.0027	0.7529	−2.2281	−0.5	0	0.544	2.7808
x_b40s_dm	Age information	0.0037	0.655	−1.9268	−0.4943	−0.0351	0.4651	2.3514
x_b50s_dm	Age information	0.0016	0.3401	−0.8767	−0.16	−0.027	0	2.5688
x_pbank_dm	Bankruptcy judge	0.0005	0.1991	−0.5676	−0.0083	0	0	1.4324

Variable	Description						
x_pmag_dm	US magistrate	−0.0006	0.2368	−0.7241	−0.0789	0	0	1.9189
x_ageon40s_dm	Age at time of commission	−0.0046	0.7589	−2.375	−0.5867	0.0331	0.4407	2.4407
x_ageon50s_dm	Age at time of commission	0.0032	0.7617	−2.2833	−0.5872	0.0116	0.5444	2.4151
x_ageon60s_dm	Age at time of commission	−0.0012	0.3923	−0.8	−0.233	−0.1522	0	1.808
x_ageon40orless_dm	Age at time of commission	0.0025	0.3155	−0.4667	−0.1722	−0.025	0	1.8911
x_ageon70ormore_dm	Age at time of commission	0	0.0087	−0.3333	0	0	0	0.6667
x_pago_dm	Justice Department	0.0021	0.4475	−1.3636	−0.2609	−0.1111	0	2.5951
x_term_dm	Number of term	−0.0011	0.8215	−2.2807	−0.5931	0	0.5185	4.5743
x_hdem_dm	Number of Democrats in the House in year of appointment	−0.1385	33.2353	−134.1666	−20.9553	0.6782	21.1747	135.5
x_hrep_dm	Number of Republicans in the House in year of appointment	0.1567	32.4092	−131.4824	−20.6667	−0.5926	19.7923	132.6667
x_sdem_dm	Number of Democrats in the Senate in year of appointment	−0.0792	9.648	−29.2975	−6.5652	−0.3511	6.4474	33.4474
x_srep_dm	Number of Republicans in the Senate in year of appointment	0.0832	9.671	−33.4298	−6.4298	0.4348	6.6497	29.3967

Table A1 (*Continued.*)

Feature name	Description	Mean	Std	Min	25%	50%	75%	Max
x_hother_dm	Number of members of other political parties in the house in year of appointment	0.0014	0.6535	−2.3973	−0.4262	−0.053	0.4198	2.9783
x_sother_dm	Number of members of other political parties in the Senate in year of appointment	0.0042	0.5781	−8.25	−0.0789	0	0	13.3333
x_agecommi_dm	Age at time of commission	−0.0262	9.4704	−39.5588	−6.5944	−0.0079	6.4379	35.448

References

Angrist, J., G. Imbens, and D. Rubin (1996). "Identification of causal effects using instrumental variables," *Journal of Econometrics* 71(1–2), 145–160.

Arora, S., Y. Liang, and T. Ma (2017). "A simple but tough-to-beat baseline for sentence embeddings," *International Conference on Learning Representations*. https://scholar.google.com/scholar?hl=en&as_sdt=0%2C9&q=ICLR+simple+baseline&btnG=#d=gs_cit&t=1654538076793&u=%2Fscholar%3Fq%3Dinfo%3AXHz21aRyb6UJ%3Ascholar.google.com%2F%26output%3Dcite%26scirp%3D0%26hl%3Den

Athey, S., J. Tibshirani, and S. Wager (2019). "Generalized random forests" *Annals of Statistics* 47(2), 1148–1178.

Bakhturina, E., N. Barry, L. Buchanan, and D. L. Chen (2016). "Events unrelated to crime predict criminal sentence length." May 1 .

Becker, S. O. (2016). "Using instrumental variables to establish causality," *IZA World of Labor*. April 1. https://wol.iza.org/articles/using-instrumental-variables-to-establish-causality/long.

Benabou, R., and J. Tirole (2011). "Law and norms," *NBER Working Paper No. 17579.*

Bengio, Y., H. Schwenk, J.-S. Senécal, F. Morin, and J.-L. Gauvain (2000). "A neural probabilistic language models," *Advances in Neural Information Processing Systems* 13.

Benson, B. L., and P. R. Zimmerman (2010). *Handbook on the economics of crime.* Edward Elgar.

Bhuller, M., and H. Sigstad (2022). "Feedback and Learning: The Causal Effects of Reversals on Judicial Decision-Making." *Available at SSRN 4000424.*

Bhuller, Manudeep and Sigstad, Henrik. (2021). Feedback and Learning: The Causal Effects of Reversals on Judicial Decision-Making (January 4, 2022). Available at SSRN: https://ssrn.com/abstract=4000424 or http://dx.doi.org/10.2139/ssrn.4000424

Bishop, C. M. (2006). *Pattern recognition and machine learning.* Springer.

Chen, Daniel L. and J. Frankenreiter. (2021). Judicial Compliance in District Courts. Available at SSRN: https://ssrn.com/abstract=4058024 or http://dx.doi.org/10.2139/ssrn.4058024

Cameron, C.M. (1993). New avenues for modeling judicial politics. In Prepared for delivery at the Conference on the Political Economy of Public Law, Rochester, NY.

Chen, D. L., J. Frankenreiter, and S. Yeh (2017). "Judicial compliance in district courts." https://ssrn.com/abstract=2740594.

Chen, Daniel L., and Markus Loecher (2019). "Mood and the malleability of moral reasoning." Available at SSRN 2740485.

Chen, D. L., V. Levonyan, and S. Yeh (2016). "Do policies affect preferences? Evidence from random variation in abortion jurisprudence," *TSE Working Paper No. 16-723*.

Chernozhukov, V., D. Chetverikov, M. Demirer et al. (2016). "Double/debiased machine learning for treatment and causal parameters." arXiv:1608.00060.

Collobert, R., and J. Weston (2008). "A unified architecture for natural language processing: Deep neural networks with multitask learning," *Proceedings of the 25th International Conference on Machine Learning*, 5 July, 160–167.

Cortes, C., and V. Vapnik (1995). "Support-vector networks," *Machine Learning* 20(3), 273–297.

Cox, D. R. (1958). "The regression analysis of binary sequences," *Journal of the Royal Statistical Society: Series B (Methodological)* 20(2), 215–232.

Dippel, C., R. Gold, S. Heblich, and R. Pinto (2017). "Instrumental variables and causal mechanisms: Unpacking the effect of trade on workers and voters," *NBER Working Paper No. 23209*.

Egami, N., C. J. Fong, J. Grimmer, M. E. Roberts, and B. M. Stewart (2017). "How to make causal inferences using texts." arXiv:1802.02163.

Fearn, N. E. (2007). "A multilevel analysis of community effects on criminal sentencing," *Justice Quarterly* 22(4), 452–487. https://doi.org/10.1080/07418820500364668.

Friedman, J. H. (2001). "Greedy function approximation: A gradient boosting machine," *Annals of Statistics* 29(5), 1189–1232.

Hartford, J., G. Lewis, K. Leyton-Brown, and M. Taddy (2017). "Deep IV: A flexible approach for counterfactual prediction," *Proceedings of the 34th International Conference on Machine Learning, PMLR* 70, 1414–1423.

Huang, W. S., M. A. Finn, R. B. Ruback, and R. R. Friedmann (1996). "Individual and contextual influences on sentence lengths: Examining political conservatism," *The Prison Journal* 76, 398–419.

Ioffe, S., and C. Szegedy (2015). "Batch normalization: Accelerating deep network training by reducing internal covariate shift," *Proceedings of the 32nd International Conference on Machine Learning*, 448–456.

Kautt, P. M. (2002). "Location, location, location: Interdistrict and intercircuit variation in sentencing outcomes for federal drug-trafficking offenses," *Justice Quarterly* 19(4), 633–671. https://doi.org/10.1080/07418820200095381.

Kornhauser, Lewis A. (1993) "The normativity of law." *American Law and Economics Review* 1, 3.

Le, Q., and T. Mikolov (2014). "Distributed representations of sentences and documents." arXiv:1405.4053.

Lewis, G., and V. Syrgkanis (2018). "Adversarial generalized method of moments." arXiv:1803.07164.

Liaw, A., and M. Wiener (2002). "Classification and regression by randomForest." *R News* 2, 18–22.

Microsoft Research (2019). "EconML: A Python package for ML-based heterogeneous treatment effects estimation," Version 0.x. https://github.com/microsoft/EconML.

Mikolov, T., I. Sutskever, K. Chen, G. S. Corrado, and J. Dean (2013). "Distributed representations of words and phrases and their compositionality," *Advances in Neural Information Processing Systems* 26, 3111–3119.

Mnih, A., and G. E. Hinton (2008). "A scalable hierarchical distributed language model," *Advances in Neural Information Processing Systems* 21, 1081–1088.

Oprescu, M., V. Syrgkanis, and Z. S. Wu (2019). "Orthogonal random forest for causal inference," *Proceedings of the 36th International Conference on Machine Learning.*

Paszke, A., S. Gross, F. Massa et al. (2019). "PyTorch: An imperative style, high-performance deep learning library," *Advances in Neural Information Processing Systems* 32, 8024–8035 http://papers.neurips.cc/paper/9015-pytorch-an-imperative-style-high-performance-deep-learning-library.pdf.

Posner, Richard A (1973). "An economic approach to legal procedure and judicial administration." *The Journal of Legal Studies* 2(2), 399–458.

Quinlan, J. R. (1986). "Induction of decision trees," *Machine Learning* 1, 81–106.

Rehurek, R., and P. Sojka (2010). "Software framework for topic modelling with large corpora," *Proceedings of the LREC 2010 Workshop on New Challenges for NLP Frameworks.*

Schmitt, C. (1969). *Gesetz und Urteil: Eine Untersuchung zum Problem der Rechtspraxis.* Munich Beck.

Schmitt, C. (1985 [1923]). *The crisis of parliamentary democracy.* Trans. E. Kennedy. MIT Press.

Schmitt, C. (2005). *Political theology: Four chapters on the concept of sovereignty.* Trans. G. Schwab. University of Chicago Press.

Srivastava, N., G. Hinton, A. Krizhevsky, I. Sutskever, and R. Salakhutdinov (2014). "Dropout: A simple way to prevent neural networks from overfitting," *The Journal of Machine Learning Research* 15(1), 1929–1958.

Stepner, M. (2014). "BINSCATTER: Stata module to generate binned scatterplots." https://michaelstepner.com/binscatter/binscatter-StataConference2014.pdf

Turian, J., L. Ratinov, and Y. Bengio (2010). "Word representations: A simple and general method for semi-supervised learning," *Proceedings of the 48th Annual Meeting of the Association for Computational Linguistics* 384–394.

Van der Maaten, L., and G. Hinton (2008). "Visualizing data using t-SNE," *Journal of Machine Learning Research*, 9(11).

Acknowledgments

Daniel L. Chen acknowledges IAST funding from the French National Research Agency (ANR) under the Investments for the Future program, grant ANR-17-EUR-0010. This research has benefited from the financial support of the research foundation TSE-Partnership and ANITI funding.

Cambridge Elements ☰

Law, Economics and Politics

Series Editor in Chief
Carmine Guerriero, *University of Bologna*

Series Co-Editors
Alessandro Riboni, *École Polytechnique*
Jillian Grennan, *Duke University, Fuqua School of Business*
Petros Sekeris, *Montpellier Business School*

Series Managing Editor
Valentino Moscariello, *University of Bologna*

Series Associate Editors
Maija Halonen-Akatwijuka, *University of Bristol*
Sara Biancini, *Université de Cergy-Pontoise*
Melanie Meng Xue, *London School of Economics and Political Science*
Claire Lim, *Queen Mary University of London*
Andy Hanssen, *Clemson University*
Giacomo Benati, *Eberhard Karls University, Tübingen*

About the Series
Decisions taken by individuals are influenced by formal and informal institutions. Legal and political institutions determine the nature, scope and operation of markets, organisations, and states. This interdisciplinary series analyses the functioning, determinants, and impact of these institutions, organizing the existing knowledge and guiding future research.

Cambridge Elements ☰

Law, Economics and Politics

Elements in the Series

Printed in the United States
by Baker & Taylor Publisher Services